NORTHERN TRAVELERS
TO SIXTEENTH-CENTURY ITALY

Drawings from New England Collections

This exhibition brings together drawings from a varied and inventive group of Netherlanders who traveled to Italy for extended stays in the sixteenth century and thereby helped to revolutionize the art of their homeland. In the fifteenth century, early Netherlandish painters such as Jan van Eyck and Rogier van der Weyden had perfected a polished, veristic style of panel painting that was characterized by the inclusion of seemingly ordinary objects and an exacting imitation of the appearance of materials, naturalistic details, and the effects of light. These artists have enjoyed great fame up to the present day. By contrast, the major artistic lights of the following century, many of whom are represented in the exhibition, were often slighted after their heyday because they appeared to have abandoned their native tradition. Sixteenth-century Netherlanders undertook the arduous journey across the Alps to Venice, Florence, and Rome in unprecedented numbers to explore a vaunted new artistic movement: the Italian Renaissance. Studying both the remains of antiquity and newly minted works by their Italian counterparts that were canonized by contemporary criticism, the Netherlanders developed a new, idealized vocabulary of art featuring activated, heroically muscled figures in dramatic compositions. The aesthetic they forged is the focus of this exhibition.

The experience of the Netherlandish artists in Italy changed over the course of the century. In the first half, they traveled south relatively early in their lives for brief periods to study antiquities rather than to seek commissions, then usually returned to their homelands where they made their careers. These artists were often active participants in humanist circles flourishing in various centers of the Low Countries. The first Netherlandish artist to study ancient art first-hand and incorporate ideas and elements of its style in his own works was Jan Gossaert (ca. 1478–1532). In 1508–09, he accompanied his patron, Philip of Burgundy, on a mission to Pope Julius II expressly to draw classical sculpture. Likewise, according to the 1604 account of the Dutch biographer Karel van Mander, Pieter Coecke van Aelst (1502–1550), whose drawing of a *Crucifixion* (no. 1) is in the exhibition, undertook a trip to Italy in the 1520's to make studies of statues and architectural subjects, some thirty years before the renowned voyage of his son-in-law Pieter Bruegel. Nourishing Coecke's interest in the Renaissance was the commission that his Brussels workshop received in 1517 to weave tapestries of the *Acts of the Apostles* from cartoons by Raphael for the Sistine Chapel. Coecke's high regard for the Renaissance continued after his return, when he edited and translated the architectural treatise by Sebastiano Serlio, itself based upon the work by the ancient author Vitruvius.

Artists active in the first decades of the century stayed in Italy for increasing periods of time, often finding Northern patrons to support them. Jan van Scorel (1495–1562), represented by a drawing with an antiquicizing allegorical subject (no. 3, cover illus.), was in Venice by 1520 and, after journeying to the Holy Land, in 1523 was appointed curator of the papal antiquities collection by the Dutch pontiff Adrian VI. According to Van Mander, it was Scorel who first enlightened his fellow artists with the Italian (or Renaissance) manner, and consequently was regarded as the founder of the modern arts in the Netherlands. Scorel's student Maerten van Heemskerck (1498–1574), to whom the sheet with the allegorical subject has also been attributed,[1] filled sketchbooks with drawings after ancient and contemporary monuments in Rome from 1532 to ca. 1537. In his *Lives of the Artists* (1568), Giorgio Vasari wrote that while in Rome Heemskerck helped to design decorations for the triumphal entry of the Hapsburg Emperor Charles V in 1536. He returned to Haarlem to become a printmaker and painter renowned for his visual expression of learned humanist subjects. Vasari reports that Michiel Coxcie (1499–1592), who remained in Rome as long as nine years, was commissioned by a cardinal from Utrecht to paint two chapels in the traditional Italian medium of fresco for the Northerners' national church, adding that he imitated the Italian manner of art very well. The Italian also remarked that Coxcie was renowned for his prints, most notably depictions of the Brazen Serpent (cf. no. 2).

By mid-century, the work of Northerners was so sought after that many artists did not return to the Netherlands and instead had profitable careers abroad. The *Temptation of Christ* (no. 18) by

Pauwels Franck (Paolo Fiammingo) (1540–1596) and the *Allegory of January* and *Allegory of May* (nos. 19 and 20) by Lodewyck Toeput (Pozzoserrato) (1550–1603/5) are drawings by artists who made their living in Northern Italy as specialists in landscape, a traditional subject of expertise for Northerners. Both artists worked for some time as landscapists in the workshop of the Venetian painter Tintoretto, as did Maerten de Vos (1532–1603). The latter artist, represented here by three drawings (nos. 10–12), returned home after four years to become a major figure in late sixteenth-century Antwerp.

Among those painters who stayed in Italy, many received commissions of importance equal to those of their Italian counterparts, executing monumental religious and historical narratives. Hans Speeckaert (ca. 1530–ca. 1577), whose *Lot and his Daughters* (no. 14) is included in the show, died a respected figure painter in Rome. Two figure studies for extant altarpieces by Denys Calvaert (1540–1619) (nos. 16, illus., and 17), an Antwerp artist who spent much of

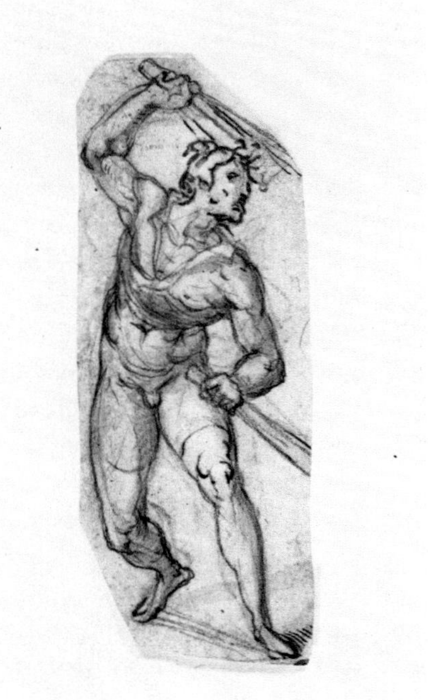

No. 16
Denys Calvaert (1540–1619)
Study of a Man for a Flagellation

3

his career in Bologna, also illustrate this trend. Other artists were known for their sponsorship by powerful patrons. Both Jan van der Straet (1523–1605) and Friedrich Sustris (ca. 1540–1599) worked in collaboration with Vasari for the Medici court in Florence in the 1560's. This patronage led to their employment in other European centers; for instance, Sustris was called to Bavaria, where he worked for Crown Prince Wilhelm (later Duke Wilhelm V). His *Allegory of Peace* (no. 13) was in all likelihood a preparatory study for a painting in one of the prince's palaces.[2] Bartholomäus Spranger (1546–1611), originally from Antwerp, was employed from 1566 to 1575 by Cardinal Alessandro Farnese and Pope Pius V. The favor of these prestigious patrons surely contributed to the artist's subsequent employment by the Hapsburg Emperors Maximilian II and Rudolf II in Vienna and Prague. Spranger's drawing of *Juno, Jupiter and Mercury* (no. 21) is related to paintings in the Prague castle.[3]

Although each artist had a marked personal style, a notable change in the manner of executing drawings took place over the course of the century. The early part of the century features compositions drawn primarily with pen and ink, in which shading is achieved by dense cross-hatching, such as Coxcie's *Brazen Serpent* (no. 2) and the sheet attributed to Scorel and Heemskerck (no. 3, cover illus.). Later drawings, such as Floris' *Fall of Phaeton* (no. 6) and De Vos' *Jonah Thrown Overboard* (no. 12, illus.), stress a more fluid movement of light and shade over a surface by means of rich chalk strokes, white highlighting, and gentle tonal washes. Toeput's allegories of the months (nos. 19 and 20) and Van den Broeck's *Allegory with the Hours and Fates* (no. 9), provide coloristic effects evoked by wash or tinted paper. The sharp, blunt pen strokes and cross-hatching characteristic of the earlier technique, already employed by Gossaert in his drawings after antiquities, serve to cast the figures into sharp relief. This drawing style is characteristic of Italian drawings for and after sculpture. Because it coincides with the strong antiquarian interests of the early sixteenth-century Netherlandish travelers to Italy, these draftsmen may well have employed the style to give a sculptural presence *all'antica* to their compositions. Later artists preferred a manner that lent more painterly qualities—

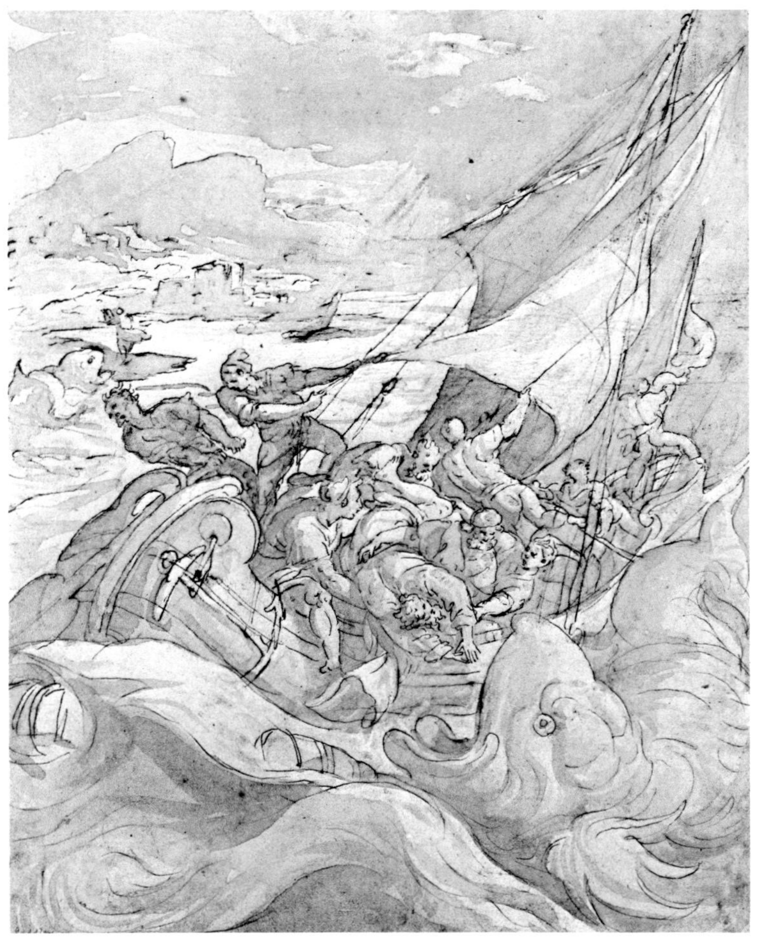

No. 12
Maerten de Vos (1532–1603)
Jonah Thrown Overboard

subtly shaded transitions between light and dark, and color—to their drawings. Heemskerck was an intermediary figure between the two trends, for he tempered the earlier, harder pen and ink style to suggest the delicate, transitory motion of light (see *Jonah Fleeing from the Presence of the Lord to Joppa,* no. 5, illus.).[4]

The artists who worked and settled in Italy did not divorce themselves from their Northern roots. On the contrary, they continuously sent their works—most notably, drawings for prints—across the Alps, so that there was a rich interchange and, ultimately, little distinction between the art they were developing in Italy and art in the Low Countries. Written sources as well as physical evidence help to define the kinds of artistic qualities Netherlanders sought in their search for a new style. Lambert Lombard (1506–1566), antiquarian and teacher of Frans Floris (1516–1570), wrote Vasari in 1565 in praise of Albrecht Dürer whose art, he maintained, was consonant with the great works of antiquity. In Lombard's view, the German Dürer, who had himself earlier studied in Italy, led the way to the perfection of art through a vigorous rather than dry manner that was intimately connected with an understanding of geometry, optics, rule and figural proportion.[5]

Lambert Lombard's evaluation of Dürer, who had introduced aspects of Renaissance style to the Netherlands through his prints and a treatise on human proportions, points to two significant features of sixteenth-century Netherlandish art. First, it emphasizes the importance of following the correct and divinely determined rules underlying nature that Renaissance artists believed they had revived from antiquity. Lombard also stressed the necessity for the appearance of vigor in figures. Indeed, Jan Gossaert's drawings after ancient sculptures already display an unmistakable bulging muscularity that enables the figures to twist actively in space; essentially, they appear to be living beings rather than stone. These qualities are a continuing feature of Netherlandish sixteenth-century art, clearly visible in the pathetically contorted victims in Coxcie's *Brazen Serpent* (no. 2) and culminating in the superhuman *Neptune* by Jan Muller (1571–1628) near the end of the century (no. 24). The departure from a naturalistic figure canon and embrace of exaggerated movement

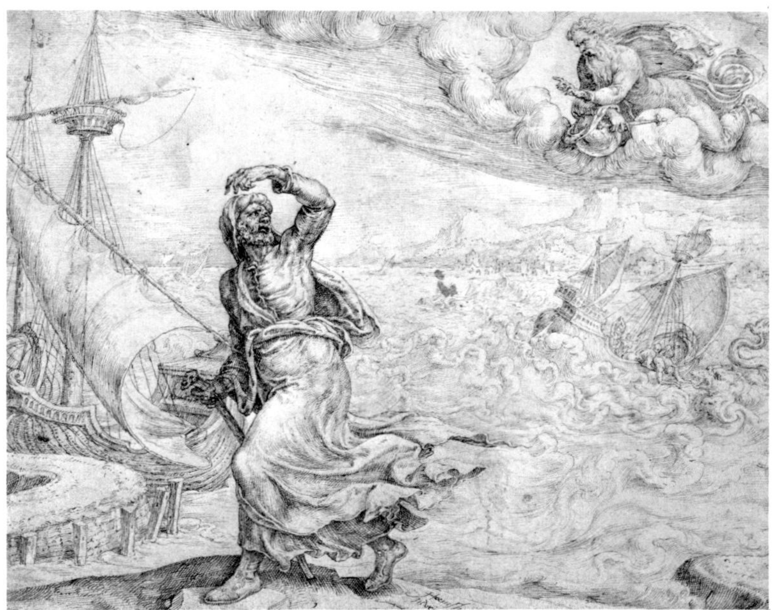

No. 5
Maerten van Heemskerck (1498–1574)
Jonah Fleeing from the Presence of the Lord to Joppa

has often been called Mannerist, the term employed for the hyper-idealized, elegant, artificial style of much Italian art immediately following the High Renaissance.[6] In view of the strong antiquarian interests of the first part of the century, however, the vigorous motion characteristic of this style might also be understood as a way of avoiding the dry quotation of motifs from ancient sources. Instead, these artists may have been seeking to interpret what they considered the main principles underlying antique art, that is, to give inanimate form the impression of life.[7]

A second item of note in Lombard's letter is that he lauds Dürer, a fellow Northerner, for exhibiting exemplary artistic qualities *all'antica* rather than praising an Italian Renaissance master such as the widely admired Michelangelo. This choice not only acknowledges the real influence of Dürer in transmitting elements of Renaissance style to the Low Countries, but also expresses the

Netherlanders' emphatic pride in their own regional heritage. Both Lombard and Van Mander place Jan van Eyck and Rogier van der Weyden in the forefront of the artistic revival there. In fact, throughout the sixteenth century, artists who embraced the "modern" manner still occasionally executed works in the archaic, revered style of their Netherlandish predecessors. Coxcie, for example, copied Van Eyck's Ghent Altarpiece for Emperor Philip II, and Heemskerck and De Vos repeated canonical subjects from the earlier era, such as St. Luke Painting the Virgin, with similarly glowing colors and a highly polished finish.

Consequently, it is not surprising that certain artistic principles derived from Northern art inform the new sixteenth-century aesthetic. Drawings offer an excellent opportunity to examine these qualities, for while Netherlandish artists clearly borrowed important ideas and techniques from their southern contemporaries, in certain significant ways their art is distinct from Italian art. Both tendencies are evident in this exhibition. For instance, Northerners often followed the working process developed by Italian Renaissance artists, whereby a sequence of drawings was made for different stages in the creation of a finished work of art. An artist's first thoughts about a composition, called *primi pensieri,* are set down in hasty, incomplete strokes, and a number of ideas are frequently sketched on a single sheet, as exemplified by the *verso* of the drawing attributed to Scorel or Heemskerck (no. 3, illus.). Subsequently, an artist would make a more detailed study from a model posing in the exact position that a figure would assume in a composition; two drawings by Denys Calvaert (nos. 16, illus., and 17) are rare examples of such figure studies by a Northern artist. Finally, fully developed compositions, or *modelli,* indicate the positions of all the figures in relation to one another, the setting, and the fall of light for the final work. De Vos' *Jonah Thrown Overboard* (no. 12, illus.) is one such *modello,* and Van der Straet's *Christ among the Doctors* (no. 7) is evidently a late compositional study for a lost painting.[8] These drawings can be squared in chalk for transfer of the design to a larger surface (e.g. *Allegory of Peace* by Sustris, no. 13).

The vast majority of preserved sheets by sixteenth-century

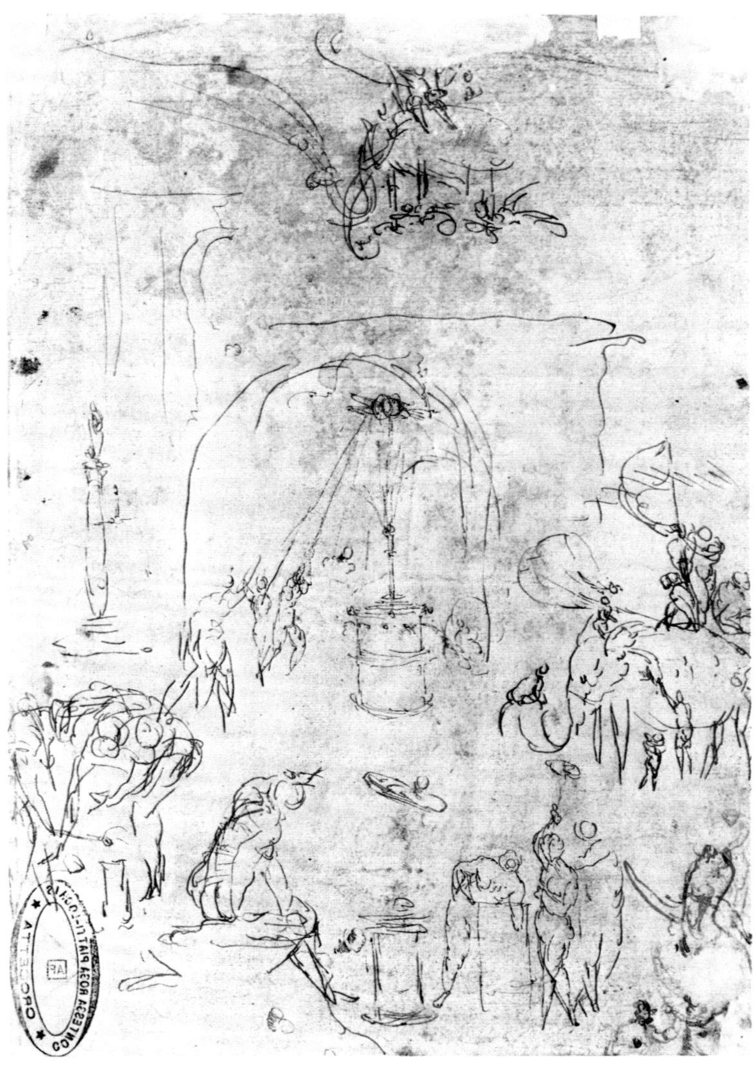

No. 3 (verso)
Jan van Scorel (1495–1562) or Maerten van Heemskerck (1498–1574)
Figure Studies

Northern masters, like those in the exhibition, are highly finished drawings rather than sketches or intermediary studies.[9] Unlike Italian drawings, they generally do not reveal different stages of the working process by means of chalk or lightly outlined pen underdrawing. This circumstance may indicate that in the North, making visible the process, or act of creation, in a drawing was not as valued as the appearance of completeness and the attendant suggestion of perfection.

This attitude, the exact opposite of the frequently voiced Italian appreciation for an emerging artistic idea expressed in mutating, sketchy form, continues an aesthetic practiced by the sixteenth-century Netherlanders' predecessors. The few preserved drawings by early Netherlandish artists resemble finished works of art, for they rarely reveal a change of mind through corrections and often painstakingly reproduce surface detail by means of a tight web of tiny strokes. Later sources expressed a high regard for perfect execution, which they identified with artistic genius. Van Mander praised the brilliance of an artist who could produce a finished pen drawing without intermediary steps, and a German connoisseur suggested that a pure pen drawing was more precious than a painting because of the greater difficulty of executing it without correction.[10]

The Netherlanders' love of finish and the appearance of instantly achieved perfection that it implies often makes it difficult to determine the function of a drawing, for stylistic qualities no longer aid in the identification of different types, as is more often the case in Italian art. Finished drawings could be either *modelli* or presentation drawings, that is, independent works of art for collectors. Clues other than style may indicate a relationship to a print: Jan Muller placed Neptune's trident in the left hand of the sea god (no. 24), a peculiarity that could reveal its function as a model because the printing process reverses a drawing.[11] Our frequent inability to conclude whether a drawing is a study or an independent work of art suggests that many drawings, including *modelli,* served a dual function both as models and, after this purpose was satisfied, as collectors' items.

Finally, the general custom of drawing in a style that could be reproduced exactly in prints heightens the natural affinity — and rivalry — between the two graphic media. This relationship is also part of a characteristically Northern aesthetic. Prints were a burgeoning art form in the sixteenth century, and virtually all of the artists in the exhibition drew for commercial publishers in the Netherlands. Actual drawings for known prints include Van der Straet's *Storks Fighting Snakes* (no. 8), Heemskerck's *Choleric Temperament* (no. 4) and his *Jonah Fleeing from the Presence of the Lord to Joppa* (no. 5, illus.), and De Vos' *The Angel Showing St. John the Heavenly City of Jerusalem* (no. 10), all of which bear the marks of tracing for transfer to the plate. By the end of the century there was a rage for pen drawings executed in the linear style of engravings, and it is likely that this reverence for a print style in draftsmanship began earlier.[12] Already Coxcie's and Heemskerck's drawings (nos. 2–5) may well have been appreciated for their graphic, print-like qualities, and Spranger's and Matham's richly tonal drawings (e.g. nos. 22 and 25) must likewise have been intended to rival chiaroscuro prints even when they were not models for them.

Recognition of the unique contributions of their early Netherlandish predecessors and pride in the print media in which Northerners had long reigned supreme: these were qualities that sixteenth-century Netherlanders refused to abandon when they journeyed across the Alps. Instead, they forged a new aesthetic by synthesizing their understanding of Renaissance and antique style with a reinterpretation of their native traditions.

Nicola Courtright
Assistant Professor of Fine Arts
Amherst College

*I am grateful to David Becker, Richard Field,
Egbert Haverkamp-Begemann, Julius Held, Thomas
DaCosta Kaufmann, David A. Levine, Anne-Marie Logan,
Sue Reed, Franklin Robinson, William Robinson, Martha
Sandweiss, Ann Sievers, Miriam Stewart, and Katharine
Watson for their assistance in preparing the exhibition and essay.*

NOTES

1. Letter from Molly Faries to William Robinson, 10 Nov. 1982, Curatorial Files, Fogg Art Museum. I find the attribution to Heemskerck convincing. The subject—sibylline prediction, sacrifice, and triumph—would suggest a relationship of the drawing to Heemskerck's employment for Charles V's entry into Rome in 1536.

2. Thomas DaCosta Kaufmann, *Drawings from the Holy Roman Empire, 1540–1680: A Selection from North American Collections* (exhibition catalogue) (Princeton: Princeton University Press for the Art Museum, Princeton University, 1982), p. 118.

3. See Thomas Le Claire Kunsthandel, *Handzeichnungen und Aquarelle des 16.–19. Jahrhunderts,* I (Hamburg: Thomas Le Claire Kunsthandel, 1983), 10; and Jaromír Neumann, "Kleine Beiträge zur rudolfinischen Kunst und ihre Auswirkungen," *Umění* 18 (1970): 142–51.

4. Cf. John Oliver Hand et al., *The Age of Bruegel: Netherlandish Drawings in the Sixteenth Century* (exhibition catalogue) (Cambridge, Eng. and New York: Cambridge University Press for the National Gallery of Art, Washington, 1986), pp. 193–95.

5. Wolfgang Krönig, "Lambert Lombard—Beiträge zu seinem Werk und zu seiner Kunstauffassung," *Wallraf-Richartz-Jahrbuch* 26 (1974): 110–11.

6. See J. Richard Judson, "Jan Gossaert, the Antique and the Origins of Mannerism in the Netherlands," in *Netherlandish Mannerism: Papers Given at a Symposium in Nationalmuseum Stockholm, September 21–22, 1984,* ed. Görel Cavalli-Björkman (Stockholm: Nationalmuseum, 1985), pp. 15–20.

7. Ernst Gombrich, "The Style *all'antica:* Imitation and Assimilation," in *The Renaissance and Mannerism: Studies in Western Art,* vol. 2, *Acts of the Twentieth International Congress of the History of Art* (Princeton: Princeton University Press, 1963), pp. 31–41.

8. Egbert Haverkamp-Begemann and Anne-Marie S. Logan, *European Drawings and Watercolors in the Yale University Art Gallery 1500–1900* (New Haven and London: Yale University Press, 1970), pp. 277–78; David P. Becker, *Old Master Drawings at Bowdoin College* (exhibition catalogue) (Brunswick, Me.: Bowdoin College Museum of Art, 1985), p. 13.

9. William W. Robinson and Martha Wolff, "The Function of Drawings in the Netherlands in the Sixteenth Century," in Hand et al., *Age of Bruegel,* p. 25.

10. Julius S. Held, "The Early Appreciation of Drawings," in *Latin American Art, and the Baroque Period in Europe: Studies in Western Art,* vol. 3, *Acts of the Twentieth International Congress of the History of Art* (Princeton: Princeton University Press, 1963), pp. 82–83; and Robinson and Wolff, pp. 36–37.

11. E.K.J. Reznicek, "Jan Harmensz. Muller as Draughtsman: Addenda," *Master Drawings* 18 (1980): 116.

12. Held, p. 83; and Robinson and Wolff, pp. 36–37.

FURTHER BIBLIOGRAPHY

Sachs, Paul J., and Mongan, Agnes. *Drawings in the Fogg Museum of Art.* Cambridge, Mass.: Harvard University Press, 1940.

Van Mander, Karel. *Het Schilderboeck . . .* Haarlem: Paschier van Wesbvach, 1604.

Vasari, Giorgio, *Le Vite de' più eccelenti pittori scultori ed architettori . . .* [1568] Ed. Gaetano Milanesi. Florence: G. C. Sansoni, 1879–1906.

EXHIBITION CHECKLIST

N.B. Dates are given to drawings when there is some scholarly consensus as to their date of execution. Only autograph inscriptions are noted.

PIETER COECKE VAN AELST (1502–1550; Italy ca. 1525)

1. *Crucifixion*, ca. 1534

   Pen and brown ink, bistre wash, and white heightening; 231 x 162 mm

   Fogg Art Museum, Harvard University, Cambridge, Massachusetts, Bequest of Charles A. Loeser. 1932.198

MICHIEL COXCIE (1499–1592; Italy ca. 1530–39)

2. *Brazen Serpent*, ca. 1534

   Pen and brown ink; 206 x 327 mm

   Fogg Art Museum, Harvard University, Cambridge, Massachusetts, Curatorial Study Group Fund, Marian H. Phinney Fund, William C. Heilman Fund, and the Paul J. Sachs Memorial Fund. 1982.50

JAN VAN SCOREL (1495–1562; Italy 1518–23) or **MAERTEN VAN HEEMSKERCK** (1498–1574; Italy 1532–ca. 1537)

3. Recto: *Allegorical Subject* / Verso: *Figure Studies*, ca. 1523 or ca. 1536

   Pen and brown ink; 309 x 219 mm

   Fogg Art Museum, Harvard University, Cambridge, Massachusetts, Paul Geier Fund. 1982.42

MAERTEN VAN HEEMSKERCK (1498–1574; Italy 1532–ca. 1537)

4. *The Choleric Temperament*, 1565

   Pen and brown ink; traced for transfer; 210 x 240 mm

   Signed and dated: *Heemskerck 1565*

   Yale University Art Gallery, Everett V. Meeks, B.A. 1901, Fund. 1964.9.4

5. *Jonah Fleeing from the Presence of the Lord to Joppa*, 1566

   Pen and brown ink; traced for transfer; 200 x 247 mm

   Signed and dated: *Heemskerck / Inventor / 1566*

   Museum of Fine Arts, Boston, Gift of Dr. Hans Schaeffer. 55.27

FRANS FLORIS (1516–1570; Italy ca. 1541–47)

6. *Fall of Phaeton*, ca. 1555

   Brush and brown ink, and black chalk; 130 x 109 mm

   Bowdoin College Museum of Art, Brunswick, Maine. 1811.108

JAN VAN DER STRAET (STRADANUS) (1523–1605;
Italy 1547–d. Florence)

7. *Christ Among the Doctors*, ca. 1570

   Brush and brown ink, brown wash, and black chalk; 409 x 278 mm

   Bowdoin College Museum of Art, Brunswick, Maine. 1811.129

8. *Storks Fighting Snakes*, 1596/1602

   Pen and brown ink, brown wash, and white heightening; traced for
   transfer; 181 x 268 mm

   Bowdoin College Museum of Art, Brunswick, Maine. 1956.24.266

CRISPIJN VAN DER BROECK (1524–before 1591; Italy before 1559)

9. *Allegory with the Hours and Fates*

   Pen and brush, black ink, black chalk, and white heightening
   (on blue-grey paper); 432 x 401 mm

   Bowdoin College Museum of Art, Brunswick, Maine. 1930.223

MAERTEN DE VOS (1532–1603; Italy ca. 1552–56)

10. *The Angel Showing St. John the Heavenly City of Jerusalem*, by 1579

    Pen and brown ink, brown wash, and white heightening; traced for
    transfer; 168 x 248 mm

    Museum of Fine Arts, Boston, Francis Welch Fund. 1985.345

11. *Three Angels*, 1583

    Pen and brown ink, brown and grey wash, and white heightening;
    traced for transfer; 188 x 292 mm

    Signed and dated: *M D VOS F 1583*

    Fogg Art Museum, Harvard University, Cambridge, Massachusetts,
    Anonymous Gift. 1978.74

12. *Jonah Thrown Overboard*, by 1589

    Pen and brown ink, brown wash, black chalk, and white heightening;
    280 x 223 mm

    Yale University Art Gallery, Library Transfer. 1961.65.51

FRIEDRICH SUSTRIS (ca. 1540–1599; b. Italy; 1568 to Bavaria; d. Munich)

13. *Allegory of Peace*, 1570's

Pen and black ink, grey wash, and black chalk; squared for transfer; 197 x 97 mm

Bowdoin College Museum of Art, Brunswick, Maine. 1811.15

HANS SPEECKAERT (ca. 1530–ca. 1577; d. Rome)

14. *Lot and His Daughters*, before 1575

Pen and brown ink, brown wash, and black chalk; 203 x 292 mm

Yale University Art Gallery, Everett V. Meeks, B.A. 1901, Fund. 1967.47.2

DENYS CALVAERT (1540–1619; Italy ca. 1562–d. Bologna)

15. *St. Jerome in the Wilderness*

Black chalk, brown wash, and white heightening (on blue paper); 265 x 211 mm

Fogg Art Museum, Harvard University, Cambridge, Massachusetts, Gift of Emile Wolf. 1986.371

16. *Study of a Man for a Flagellation*, ca. 1572/75

Pen and black ink, and red chalk; 126 x 49 mm

Collection Julius S. Held

17. *Study of an Angel*

Pen and grey ink, and black chalk; 239 x 102 mm

Yale University Art Gallery, Library Transfer. 1961.66.55

PAUWELS FRANCK (PAOLO FIAMMINGO) (1540–1596; Italy before 1573–d. Venice)

18. *Temptation of Christ*

Pen and brown ink; 255 x 198 mm

Yale University Art Gallery, Library Transfer. 1961.62.39

LODEWYCK TOEPUT (POZZOSERRATO) (1550–1603/5; Italy ca. 1573–d. Treviso)

19. *Allegory of January*, 1580's/90's

Pen and grey-black ink, brown and blue wash, and graphite; 274 x 415 mm

Yale University Art Gallery, Library Transfer. 1961.63.65

20. *Allegory of May*, 1580's/90's

Pen and grey ink, grey and blue wash; 273 x 416 mm

Yale University Art Gallery, Library Transfer. 1961.63.67

BARTHOLOMÄUS SPRANGER (1546–1611; Italy 1566–75)

21. *Juno, Jupiter and Mercury*, ca. 1585

Pen and brown ink, grey-brown wash, and white heightening;
204 x 199 mm

Signed: *B / Sprangers antvers / inventor*

Fogg Art Museum, Harvard University, Cambridge, Massachusetts,
Purchase in honor of Konrad Oberhuber with funds presented by an
anonymous donor. 1983.142

22. *Mars and Venus*, 1597

Pen and brown ink, grey wash, and white heightening; 260 x 210 mm

Dated: *1597*

Smith College Museum of Art, Northampton, Massachusetts. 1963:52

23. *Venus and Mercury*

Pen and brown ink, brown and grey wash, and white heightening;
370 x 253 mm

Yale University Art Gallery, Enoch Vine Stoddard, B.A. 1905, Fund.
1974.38

JAN MULLER (1571–1628; Italy 1594–ca. 1602)

24. *Neptune*, ca. 1589

Pen and brown ink, brown wash, white heightening, and black chalk;
421 x 291 mm

Yale University Art Gallery, Everett V. Meeks, B.A. 1901, Fund.
1963.9.75

JACOB MATHAM (1571–1631; Italy ca. 1593–99)

25. *St. Joseph as Carpenter*

Pen and brown ink, grey and white heightening, and graphite; traced
for transfer; 205 x 178 mm

Museum of Fine Arts, Boston, Gift of Maida and George Abrams.
1986.921

26. *Ruins on the Palatine Hill* (attributed), 1590's

Pen and brown ink, brown, blue, red and green wash; 417 x 300 mm

Worcester Art Museum, Worcester, Massachusetts. 1956.22

UNKNOWN FLEMISH ARTIST

27. *Ruins of the Baths of Diocletian*, 1590/1600
    Pen and brown ink; 276 x 431 mm
    Inscribed: *Termina deoclesiano*
    Yale University Art Gallery, Library Transfer. 1961.64.16

PHOTOGRAPH CREDITS

No. 3 recto (cover) and verso, Fogg Art Museum, Harvard University;
no. 5, Museum of Fine Arts, Boston; no. 12, Yale University Art Gallery;
no. 16, Sterling and Francine Clark Art Institute.